Birds

Owls

GARY DICKINSON

GARY DICKINSON

Copyright © 2012 Gary Dickinson

ISBN: 1495241726
ISBN-13: 978-1495241727

DEDICATION

My father-in-law loved owls so when my wife asked me
if I would write a book about owls and to dedicate it to him,
it was something easily done.

This book therefore,
is written for and on behalf of my wife,
dedicated to her father and my dear father-in-law, Les,
who loved owls.

CONTENTS

ACKNOWLEDGMENTS

All information in this book has been carefully researched and checked for factual accuracy. However, the authors and publishers make no warranty, express or implied, that the information contained herein is appropriate for every individual, situation or purpose, and assume no responsibility for errors or omissions. The reader assumes the risk and full responsibility for all actions, and the authors will not be held responsible for any loss or damage, whether consequential, incidental, special or otherwise that may result from the information presented in this publication.

We have relied on our own experience as well as many different sources for this book, and we have done our best to check facts and to give credit where it is due. In the event that any material is incorrect or has been used without proper permission, please contact us so that the oversight can be corrected.

Photos are purchased stock photography

or are licensed under a Creative Commons Attribution Sharealike 2.0 Generic License
http://creativecommons.org/licenses/by-sa/2.0/

Chapter 1

AMAZING OWLS

A wise old owl sat on an oak;
The more he saw the less he spoke;
The less he spoke, the more he heard;
Why aren't we like that wise old bird?
Charles M Schulz

The fascination with owls goes back to time immemorial. In some cultures, the owl is a symbol of wisdom and yet to others, they are a forewarning of doom and even imminent death.

In Sicily for example, it is believed that the Common Scops Owl will sing for three days near the house of a person who is about to die.

Common Scops Owl

What is it about the owl that holds such mystery and fascination? What does the owl mean to you? What do you know about the owl – where it lives; what it eats; how it hunts; how it sees and hears so well; how it flies so silently; how big, or small, does the owl get…

Outlined in this book are a few interesting facts and some insights for you to come to your own conclusion as to whether you think the owl is a symbol of wisdom or rather a bird to avoid altogether for fear of imminent doom and gloom.

Fact: Did you know that a group of owls is called a parliament?

Chapter 2

A WISE OLD OWL SAT IN AN OAK

There is such a wide variety of owls, large, small and anything in-between. There is bit of a contest for the largest of them with 5 owls being in the largest category. The top 5 are: -

Eurasian Eagle Owl

1. Eurasian Eagle Owl
2. Great Grey Owl
3. Snowy Owl
4. Great Horned Owl
5. Blakiston's Fish Owl

Great Horned Owl

It is generally accepted though that the Eurasian Eagle Owl tops them where the larger females, weighing up to 9lbs with a wingspan topping 7ft across, takes first prize.

The smallest of the owls goes to a choice of 2. The toss up is between: -

Elf Owl
Courtesy Peter Wilton @ Flickr.com

1. The Elf Owl, and
2. The Northern Pygmy Owl

While both can qualify as the smallest, the Elf Owl is generally accepted as the smallest weighing in at approximately 1.4oz

Northern Pygmy Owl
Courtesy David-Mitchell @ Flickr.com

Big or small, all owls appear to have a face. This "face" is called a facial disc and feathers from the facial disc cover their ears as well as their beak.

Most owls are active between the hours of dusk and dawn, so for an owl, having spent the day-time very quietly and inconspicuously resting, or in owl speak, roosting, "wake-up" time for them is the end of the day as we know it.

Owls are not unlike us as humans when we wake up in the morning. Just as we get up in the morning and start to ready ourselves for the day, so does the owl.

We might give a good stretch before swinging our legs out of bed and making our way to the bathroom followed by a yawn. We'll have a shower, ruffle our hair (okay, wash it) by which time we're awake enough to sing our favorite song while washing and scrubbing ourselves. We hop out the shower, dry ourselves, brush our hair and noticing that our nails need a trim, if we're nail biters, our teeth do the job for us and if not, we clip them.

Similarly, the owl starts its day (night) with a stretch and a yawn. It then proceeds to preen (wash) itself after which it combs its head (brushes its hair) with its claws. It ruffles its feathers as if drying itself and then cleans its claws and toes by nibbling them with its beak. "Ablutions" done, it hops off the roost and if in the mood, gives a hoot (song) especially if he's keen for a date i.e. it's breeding season. How similar is that to the start of our day!

Wet Eagle Owl

Fact: Owls do actually bathe. They do this in the rain (okay perhaps not a lot of choice in that case), but they do also bathe in shallow water.

Quite understandably, you could be forgiven for thinking that owls just sit in a tree (or similar) all day and come alive at night and even then that's an assumption only because we may be lucky to hear an owl hooting let alone seeing one.

Quite often though, they break this mould of "seriousness" and you might see them bobbing and weaving their heads almost as if they are curious about something.

Barred Owl

There is method in their madness, as it's a way for the owl to further improve its already incredible three-dimensional understanding of what they are viewing.

Relaxed Barn Owl Basking In Sunlight

If you want to know if an owl is relaxed, just look at its plumage (feathers). If it looks loose and fluffy, then you're looking at a relaxed bird. If its feathers are pulled right up against the body and if they have any ear tufts, they are standing straight up, then the owl is likely to be alarmed.

In addition to this, when alarmed, some owls will cock their tail and flick it from side to side. A little like a cat does when it's agitated. A pygmy owl is an example of an owl with this behavior.

Cuban Pygmy Owl

Typical postures when feeling threatened, owls will ruffle their feathers so as to make them appear much larger than they really are. They might lower their head and spread their wings out with the leading edge pointing down. Almost like presenting a shield toward its apparent threat. Added to this, they might make clicking noises with their tongues.

Fact: some species of owls, when nesting, have been known to exhibit quite aggressive behavior toward humans going so far as attacking them. Snowy owls are an example of exhibiting this kind of behavior.

Male and Female Snowy Owls

This may sound surprising, but not all owls hoot. There is actually quite a range of sounds that owls make. The best known is probably the hoot but they are also known to give eerie screeches and screams, and they also whistle, purr, hiss, snort, chitter and even make clicking noises with their tongues.

Owls are not really migratory birds although there are some that do escape the harsh winters of the north by moving south.

Chapter 3

WHAT DO OWLS EAT?

Being birds of prey, owls feed on other animals. These can be anything from spiders, snails, crabs, fish, frogs to other birds to small mammals like hares.

Great Grey Owl

As you can imagine, the size and nature of the diet is dependent on the size of the owl. Barn owls for instance feed on mice and shrews. Large Eagle Owls feed upon hares and young foxes, birds like ducks and other game birds. Fish owls such as the African Fishing Owl prey upon fish as the name implies.

Two Juvenile Brown Fish Owls

Owls generally roost during the day and hunt during the night but their "hunting grounds" are usually not the same area as their day time roosting spot.

When it comes to hunting, owls are a little like stealth fighter planes because the first you know they're there it's already too late. Owls are very efficient hunters. Their eyes allow them to see on the dimmest of nights. Their hearing is adept at helping them locating prey that would otherwise be totally concealed. Some owls can even locate unsuspecting prey in complete darkness. Having located their prey, they need to then swoop upon their prey without it knowing what hit it so that there is no chance of it escaping. Its flight is silenced by having special wing feathers that muffle the sound of the air rushing over its wings that would otherwise give it away.

Great Horned Owl In Flight

All of those special adaptations together make the owl a lethal weapon to any unsuspecting prey not only because they allow the owl to find its prey with pinpoint accuracy but it's able to make any adjustments while in flight as it picks up any movement by the unaware prey.

More often than not, owls swoop down onto their prey with open wings and talons outstretched in front of them. They do this from their perch which could be a branch, a tree stump or even a fence post. Being extremely efficient gliders, some glide a little way from their perch while others drop straight down from their perch stretching out their wings at the last moment. However they do it, the prey has very little chance, if any, to escape as can be seen in the picture below.

Short Eared Owl With Mouse

There are a few species that prefer to soar above while scanning below for suitable food. Once located, the owl flies directly toward it keeping its head in line with it thus detecting any movements by the target. At the last moment the owl pulls its head back and thrusts its feet forward with talons spread out wide to latch onto its prey. Quite often the force of the impact will stun the prey but no sooner captured, the owl completes the task of killing its prey with its sharp, strong beak.

Bengal Eagle Owl

Depending on the kind of prey being hunted, owls can certainly change the way they hunt. For example, owls can flush birds or insects from their tree cover only to be caught mid air, or, similar to fish eagles, some owls like the Pel's Fishing Owl, can catch fish on the fly snatching them from the water as they skim passed. Other "fishing owls" like the Blakiston's Fish Owl prefer to perch at the water's edge grabbing any unsuspecting fish that ventures too close to the surface.

Blakiston's Fish Owl
Courtesy Robert tdk @ Flickr.com

Whichever method its prey is caught, the quarry is eaten immediately if small enough; carried away in its bill or if too large to carry in its bill, it is carried in its talons to a safe perch. Sometimes owls cover or shield their prey with their wings. This is probably to hide it from other possible predators that might want to steal it. The posture that they adopt when covering their prey is called mantling.

Chapter 4

THE MORE HE SAW THE LESS HE SPOKE

An owl's eyes are striking and aside from the fact that they are so large they are also forward facing. Perhaps this is what makes an owl appear so wise! But having forward facing eyes has an added advantage for the owl. It also allows it to see objects with both eyes at the same time. This is something called binocular vision. So what's the big deal about that you may ask? Well, it means that owls can see objects in the same way humans do (height, width and depth). They can even judge distance the same way.

Spectacled Owl

Remembering that owls hunt between dusk and dawn (low light – darkness) their large eyes means that they are extremely efficient at seeing under these conditions of low light.

Fact: Owls cannot roll or move their eyes. They can only look straight ahead.

So we have an owl that has binocular vision and can only look straight ahead. Sounds fairly limiting wouldn't you think? It is but then the owl has something up its sleeve to more than compensate for this apparent limitation. It can turn its head 135 degrees in either direction (left or right) giving it a total of 270 degrees "field of view". It can even turn its head almost upside down.

Barn Owl

You could be forgiven for thinking that owls have very sensitive eyes in the daytime when light conditions are bright. Just like us though, owls also have a pupil that has a wide range of adjustment which controls the amount of light that enters the eyes.

Fact: Owls have 3 eyelids.

Like us they have an upper and lower eyelid except that their upper one closes when the owl blinks. The lower one closes when the owl sleeps. The third one is called a nictitating membrane which closes across the eye. It closes from the inside (near the beak) to the outside. The purpose of this membrane (or eyelid) is to clean the surface of the eye and also to protect it.

Chapter 5

THE LESS HE SPOKE, THE MORE HE HEARD

Like the owl's eyesight, the hearing in owls is extremely well developed. As you can imagine, hunting at night requires highly sensitive and developed hearing in order to "tune in" to the slightest movements of their prey.

Fact: Not only can owls pick up the slightest movement of their prey in the leaves or undergrowth but they can also detect movements under the snow.

Eastern Screech Owl

An owl's ears are located behind their eyes on either side of their head. They are covered by the feathers of their facial disc. In some owls, it appears that they have very pronounced ears. These apparent ears are actually just display feathers that form what's called ear tufts.

Although the range of sounds that can be heard (audible sounds) are very similar to humans, the owl's hearing is far more acute particularly at specific frequencies. This is what enables them to hear just the faintest of sounds with pinpoint accuracy.

Some owls have one ear slightly higher than the other. This is particularly prevalent in those that are strictly nocturnal (hunt at night) for example the Barn Owl or Boreal Owl.

Barn Owl

You'll notice too that the facial disc in these owls is very noticeable and well defined. This facial disc can be "adjusted" at will with their facial muscles. The benefit of this is that their faces act like a radar dish directing the sounds right into the ear openings.

And just to fine tune the way sound is directed to their ears, an owl's beak is pointed down. This just enhances the effect of the "radar dish" by increasing its surface area.

Ural Owl

How exactly does the owl locate its prey then? Remember that the owl has one ear slightly higher than the other? Well, it's because of this that when an owl hears a noise, it can tell the direction that it came from due to the very slight difference in time that the sound reaches each ear. That difference is only 30 millionths of second but that's all it needs to know which direction the noise came from.

The first thing that the owls does is to turn its head toward the sound source which it repeats until the sound reaches both ears at the same time.

White Faced Owl

When this happens, the owl knows that it is facing directly toward the sound source.

Another advantage of the ears being uneven is that it also tell whether the sound is higher or lower in relation to its position.

All these sound calculations happen instantly in the owls brain where it is able to create a picture in its brain exactly where that sound comes from. So highly developed is this system that the owl is able to adjust this picture with pinpoint accuracy while flying so that if the prey is "on the move" the owl keeps totally focused on its location right up until it thrusts its legs out in front of its face with talons spread right onto its target.

Chapter 6

FEATHERS AND FLIGHT

Birds have up to five feather types and owls are no different having them all in varying degrees. Owls do however, have feathers that are specially designed such as the feathers of the facial disc that are stiff, the ear-flap feathers and the bristle like feathers around the beak.

Great Grey Owl

Remember that the owl has remarkable vision and yet is unable to see objects clearly that are too close to it? Perhaps to compensate for this, owls have feathers called filoplumes, on their feet and beaks which are used to "feel" helping the owl to react to things they touch… like the prey they may have just caught.

Patterns

Have you ever heard an owl hoot during the day but struggled to see it on its perch? Almost impossible right!

Spotted Wood Owl

Owls conceal or hide themselves with their very specific colors and patterns that they exhibit which allow it to blend in with its surroundings. Take the white snowy owl for example. It wouldn't conceal itself very well in a forest just as a Great Horned Owl wouldn't in the snowfields.

Snowy Owl

Remember that when an owl is relaxed, it takes up a puffed up appearance but if it is alarmed, or threatened in any way, it will attempt to conceal itself by compacting its feathers, closing its eyes and raising its ear tufts which it does to show what its feeling e.g. excited, angry or scared. Combining those actions all help to camouflage the owl allowing it to blend in with its surroundings.

Wash Time

Have you ever seen a bird preen itself? It looks like it's scratching itself and in a way it is, except that what it's actually doing is cleaning and grooming itself. Owls use their beak and talons a little bit like using a comb.

This act of preening removes dust, dirt and even parasites living on the bird. They clean their heads using the two outer talons.

Flight feathers, are usually locked together by little hooks (called barbules), sometimes become unhooked thus separating the feathers from each other. In order to lock the feathers together again to get them into peak condition, owls use their beaks to realign the barbules. Similar to pulling a zipper down when it comes apart and then pulling it back up again to fasten or lock the teeth together.

Silent Night; Silent Flight

The front edge of a plane's wing is referred to as the leading edge. Similarly, the front edge of the owl's wing is also called the leading edge. When a bird is in flight, air rushes over the surfaces of the wing creating turbulence as it passes over and behind the wing. The movement of this air creates a "gushing" noise that is audible.

Eagle Owl

This wouldn't serve the owl very well when it relies so much on the element of surprise when hunting. The noise would definitely be a dead giveaway for the owl.

To counteract this apparent design fault, the owl's wings have a rather special unique adaptation to the leading edge of its primary wing feathers. Owls have something called "flutings" on the leading edge of their wings – a fringe like edge which breaks down the turbulent air into little pockets of turbulent air effectively muffling the rushing air over the surfaces of the wings. The result: silent flight!

What Big Feet You Have.

For most owls, feathers cover their feet for three

reasons:

1. To keep their feet warm in cold weather,
2. To sense contact with prey held in the feet, and
3. To protect their feet from prey that might try to bite after being caught

Owls have 4 toes but the outer toe has a flexible joint that allows it to swivel to the front and to the back. When the owl is perched or clutching its prey for example, the owl has two forward facing and two backward facing toes. When it is in flight, the toe swivels forward so that three face forward and one back.

Juvenile Burrowning Owl

Since their feet are an owl's primary weaponry, their feet are also well designed for the job of killing, holding and perching. Owls generally fly right up to their prey and impact it with their outstretched feet. To withstand that force, their feet have shorter and stronger bony structures than those in other birds.

Also, the underside of their feet is rough and knobby which helps when gripping prey or when perched somewhere.

Fact: Owls are able to lock their toes around a perch or their prey without their toe muscles needing to remain contracted.

White Fronted Scops Owls

Chapter 7

15 INTERESTING, AMAZING AND FUN FACTS ABOUT OWLS

Fact # 1: *Owls are birds of prey*

Birds of prey (or raptors) are birds that feed on mammals, other birds, insects, and reptiles. Owls don't have teeth and therefore they swallow small prey whole and where their prey is too large for that, they tear it into smaller pieces in order to swallow it. They later bring up pellets of indigestible material such as bone, fur, and feathers (if it was a bird).

Fact # 2: *Owls ears are asymmetrical*

One ear is larger and set higher upon its head than the other

Fact # 3: *The Elf Owl is the smallest in the world*

It weighs approximately 1.4oz and is smaller than a house sparrow. Elf owls are also known to "play dead" when caught.

Fact # 4: *The structure of an owl's foot is referred to as zygodactyl*

Two of the toes face forward while two face backward. This arrangement is extremely useful when capturing prey since it enables it catch and hold its prey easily. It is also possible to rotate the outer back facing toe forward to give it a 3-forward, 1-back configuration which is occasionally used for perching but more often than not when flying.

Fact # 5: *Owls fly silently*

Owls primary flight feathers have a "modified" leading edge which allows them to fly by stealth virtually undetected.

Fact # 6: *Most owls are nocturnal*

This means they are active at night. Pygmy owls for example are active in the hours of early morning and/or at dusk (crepuscular). The Burrowing owl and the Short-eared owl on the other hand are active during the day.

Fact # 7: *Owls' eyes are fixed in their sockets*

Owls are unable to move their eyes within their sockets i.e. swivel them up, down or to the sides. They more than compensate for this "disability" by being able to turn their entire head 135 degrees in either direction (270 degrees in total). Contrary to popular myth, owls cannot turn its head completely backwards giving the belief that they can turn their heads a total of 360 degrees)

Fact # 8: *Owls don't only make the "hoot hoo" sound we associate with them*

The familiar hoot that we all know, is usually a territorial declaration, but not all species are able to hoot. Owls might make other sounds that could include screeches, hisses, and screams. Different sounds are made for different situations e.g. when looking for a mate or defending territory etc.

Fact # 9: *Owls mate for life!*

Fact # 10: *Most owls do not migrate*

There are some owls that escape the harsh northern winters by moving south.

Fact # 11: *Owls are farsighted*

Owls are unable to see anything that is within a few centimeters of their eyes clearly. Any prey that is securely within their grasp is sensed by touch rather than sight. Using the filoplumes (stiff bristle like feathers), that they have over the beak and feet they are able to sense their prey.

Fact # 12: *Owls have 3 eyelids*

All 3 eyelids are used for different purposes. The upper lid for example, is used when an owl blinks. The lower lid is used when sleeping. The third which is more like a thin membrane (layer of tissue) is used to clean and lubricate they eye. This lid is called a nictitating membrane and moves across the eye from the inside to the outside.

Fact # 13: *There are approximately 200 owl species*

Owls are found in all regions of the world except the poles, most of Greenland and some remote islands.

Fact # 14: *Burrowing owlets mimic a rattlesnake's rattle to scare off would be predators*

Fact # 15: *Want to know an owl's habits? Look into its eyes.*

Research suggests that the activity habits of owls determines their eye color. For example, when looking into the eyes of a black and orange eyed owl, you're more than likely looking at a nocturnal owl. If the eyes you're looking at are yellow, the owl can be both diurnal and nocturnal.

Bonus Fact: *A group of owls is called a parliament*

Burrowing Owls — Who Called This Meeting Anyway?

Chapter 8

CONCLUSION — WHY AREN'T WE LIKE THAT WISE OLD BIRD?

Wise or sinister? Owls seem to be very well adept for the task at hand i.e. keeping a low profile while roosting; when hunting, locating their prey and with laser focus dropping or flying by stealth to snatch it in their powerful talons finally finishing the job with their powerful beak. Therefore, wise because they know when to sit and watch, when to sleep, when to relax and when to hunt.

Owl Monkey

Nowhere do they fly into someone's path in an attempt to "haunt" or impose bad luck. This belief or superstition is something that has possibly been handed down from generation to generation and will continue to do so until.... well, possibly will continue to be. Therefore, sinister until the chain is broken.

Owl Butterfly

ABOUT THE AUTHOR

Gary Dickinson always felt there was at least one book 'inside him'. In 2013 he traded the corporate world for the life of a writer, and today shares his diverse interests through his children's books. His love of nature is captured in his series of books on birds, mammals, reptiles and amphibians, while his passion for planes has generated a series on aviation.

Gary's books are read and loved by children around the world, and Gary brings his stories to life to inspire a new generation of adventurers and nature lovers.

Gary's philosophy is simple: you don't need to go far for adventure - if you look closely, you'll find it right on your doorstep!

Made in the USA
San Bernardino, CA
03 April 2018